ESPERANZA and HOPE

ESPERANZA and HOPE

Esperanza Snyder

POEMS

Sheep Meadow Press
Rhinebeck, New York

For Isabella, Stephany, and William

Cover image: Francisco de Zurbarán, *The Education of the Virgin*
Author photograph: Piccadilly Posh

Library of Congress Cataloging-in-Publication Data

Names: Snyder, Esperanza, author.
Title: Esperanza and hope : poems / Esperanza Snyder.
Description: Rhinebeck, New York : Sheep Meadow Press, [2018] |
    Includes bibliographical references.
Identifiers: LCCN 2018012995 | ISBN 9781937679750 (pbk.)
Classification: LCC PS3619.N9325 A6 2018 | DDC 811/.6--dc23
LC record available at https://lccn.loc.gov/2018012995

All inquiries and permission requests should be addressed to
the publisher:

The Sheep Meadow Press
PO Box 84
Rhinebeck, NY 12514

ACKNOWLEDGMENTS

Alehouse Press: "Beyond Bogotá"

Blackbird: "Confessions for the Guerrilla Fighter Upstairs,"
"My Father's Language"

Cutthroat: A Journal of the Arts: "Blue Nights"

Fluent Magazine: "Photograph of a Man Standing by a Waterfall"

Free State Review: "Salamanca," "Swimming in Madrid," "Salamanca,
Summer Sundays," "Falling," "Plaza Santa Ana"

In Good Company Poetry Anthology: "Elegy for My Grandfather,"
"Napping with Steve Orlen," "Ingrid Betancourt after Her Release"

32 Poems: "Mercatale"

The Comstock Review: "Elegy for My Grandfather Who Died in a City
Surrounded by Mountains"

The Gettysburg Review: "In the Changing Light," "What I Never Told You
about the Marriage," "Napping with Steve Orlen," "In Mar del Plata,
Where Alfonsina Walked into the Sea," "My Father's Letter"

The Kenyon Review: "Memory in the Wine"

Poetry Society of America: "Cante Flamenco"

The Squaw Valley Review Poetry Anthology: "Elegy for Eugenio Montale"

OCHO #23: "In Bogotá"

Old Flame: From the First 10 Years of 32 Poems Magazine: "Mercatale"

Redactions: Poetry & Poetics: "Ingrid Betancourt after Her Release"

AUTHOR'S NOTE

I will be forever indebted to Stanley Moss, without whom this book would not have come into being. I am grateful to him for the many hours spent in his study reading—first my poems, then my prose, and discussing both. I am grateful for his intelligence as an editor, and for his fascinating stories, grateful for his wit, his questions, his suggestions. His magnanimous spirit and his willingness to engage in dialogue benefited not only this book, but also this writer. As early as our first meeting, Stanley suggested that I write an essay to provide context for the poems. Once, while talking about my years in Italy and Spain he asked me why my name was Hope. "Your real name," he said, "is Esperanza." His words inspired the section about my different names in the essay. Looking at my work and my life through Stanley's eyes has given me a better understanding of my role as an artist, and, more importantly, the courage to shed Hope Maxwell Snyder's clothes in order to wear those of Esperanza, Esperanza Snyder. Working with Stanley has been a transformative experience, one I will never forget. He encouraged me to take risks, to be playful, and truthful, to make clear my own history to me and my readers—he thought it best that I write under the name Esperanza because it is true to me, body and soul, my real Christian name is Esperanza. In our contract for this book, my first name is Hope. I thought the discovery is the greatest discovery since fire, the wheel, and metaphor.

I am especially grateful to Michael Collier and Stanley Plumly for reading my poems early on, as well as several drafts of the manuscript, and for making precious suggestions. I've been fortunate enough to study with other wonderful teachers who also taught me a great deal about the craft and inspired me to work hard, including Edward Hirsch, Steve Orlen, and Ellen Bryant Voigt. I want to thank them, and to thank Michael and Bread Loaf for believing in me and giving me the opportunity to share my writing with others.

Heartfelt thanks to Grace Cavalieri for her support, and to Mary and Jim Holland, Greg Miller, and William Snyder for reading the manuscript and for their intelligent recommendations.

CONTENTS

EUROPA

ESTADOS UNIDOS

POEM BY STANLEY MOSS

NOTES

WHO IS ESPERANZA SNYDER?

I've lived in three countries, married three times, had three children, two out of wedlock. I'm fluent in three languages, and conversational in a fourth. I attended five colleges, eight, if you count a summer course at the University of Salamanca, a brief stay at the University of Florence—where I was admitted as a senior, with three exams left to take before graduating with a *Laurea*—and one semester at a low residency MFA program. My first institution of "higher learning" was Montgomery College in Rockville, Maryland.

I could have been a citizen of three countries. When I left Stefano Rossi my application for Italian citizenship had been approved. I've never had a Colombian passport, but was thinking of applying for one. It took my brother months to find my birth certificate in Bogotá, which made me question my mother, since what she often tells me is inaccurate, my own birth mysterious. I've never received child support or alimony, and each time I left a husband, I took few clothes and a couple of books. I've worked in candy stores, women's boutiques, and a store that sold everything, taught at four colleges. After my promotion and tenure at Shepherd University, I took a leave of absence. I never returned, never got a sabbatical, either. While living in Italy, I taught English and sold emeralds. After returning to the States, this time with my daughter, Stephany, I used my emerald money to rent a furnished efficiency at the Topaz House in Bethesda, Maryland. But I'm getting ahead of myself.

My childhood was spent in Bogotá, my adolescence in Maryland, my twenties in Tuscany. Like my husbands, my parents came from different worlds. My mother married my father, then got to know him. She says he married her for her money—that is, my grandfather's money—and perhaps he did, since he was born in Georgia, into a Scotch-Irish family of migrant workers specializing in picking apples. He had no inheritance to speak of. My grandparents' ancestors on my mother's side traveled to the Americas from Cantabria and Granada.

When my maternal grandparents met, my grandmother was a single mother with two children. Her husband had left her. Mamá Inés and

Papá Regulo, as I called them, never married, and only lived together for a few years. Soon, he moved on. You see, he was fire, my grandmother water. He was a match—my grandmother, lake Guatavita, with a whole town immersed inside her. He was small and fast, stone striking stone, started a fire that would burn long. He worked at the railroad, sold emeralds, ended up owning a bus company, started the first tourism business in Colombia—El Dorado Turismo—bought land, built houses and apartment buildings, an empire. She had lovely legs, gave birth to six children (four with my grandfather), prayed, and died poor.

My parents too had different destinies. My father spoke English, my mother Spanish, and even though he learned to speak Spanish perfectly and she speaks English as well as she can, they never really learned each other's language. My mother met my father at the University of Alabama, where my grandfather sent her to receive an American education. She wasn't a good student, but she had a busy social life, and many admirers. In Alabama, she won a beauty contest. The men probably found her olive skin and black hair attractive. She dated fraternity boys, and, sometimes, had more than one date on the same night. Shortly after they married, not knowing what else to do, my parents moved to Colombia. My brother was born a year later. Eighteen months after that, in a bathtub filled with water at the Clinica de Marly, a team of Russian doctors presiding, I came into the world. You see, I was part of a Russian experiment introduced by Igor Charkovsky in Russia. Those of us born in bathtubs came to be known as Water Babies. When my mother first mentioned the circumstances of my birth, I thought she was making it up, since fiction is her calling, but I soon realized she was serious. I even discovered that some women give birth, not in bathtubs, but in the ocean. Oftentimes, dolphins show up during the baby's birth. I've tried to imagine my birth in that Colombian bathtub filled with warm water, my angry mother pushing me out, my father slow dancing in a club with another woman, the Russian doctors saying "push" in Russian, my maternal grandfather, who didn't like to drive, driving around the city looking for my father so he could drag him to the clinic to meet me. But the dolphins, where were the dolphins? And, why go through all that trouble trying to find my father? He was always getting lost, and would wiggle away before I was five.

You see, my father was mercury, a combination of the planet and the element, moving fast, changing, and toxic to touch. My mother was clouds threatening rain. He was hard to pin down, hard to understand. Showing my mother his large, white hands, his long fingers, he would say, "these hands will work for you!" But they didn't. He had a beautiful voice, good looks, a gift for selling. He had brains, according to my mother. He had ambition too, though he lacked the discipline to persevere. My father was over six feet tall, strong, handsome, with blue eyes and blond hair. He was always writing a book, starting new business ventures, failing. He was restless, unfulfilled potential.

I don't understand why my parents baptized me Hope, and never called me by my baptismal name. After my birth, explaining my existence to my brother, they called me Sister. Then they tried to switch to Hope, and realized no one in Colombia could pronounce that name. Because the "h" is silent in Spanish, Hope sounded like Opec without the "c" at the end. My father decided to call me Lee, after his mother, whom I never met, and I grew up answering to Lee. Some people still call me Lee, though when I moved to Maryland, Hope became my stage name. While in Colombia, in the country of my childhood, I will always be Lee, the name my father gave me before evaporating.

After my father left us, my mother, my brother, and I moved in with my maternal grandfather, his mistress Orfi, their son, her daughter, and their live-in maid. It was an unhappy household, full of bitter women who hated each other, always fighting for my grandfather's attention, always blaming. While my mother's salary from teaching at El Sagrado Corazón (Sacred Heart, a Catholic school), barely paid for our school, her job with the nuns gave her some independence. She went to work, leaving the maid and Orfi to do the cooking, cleaning, washing. Orfi's daughter, Gladys, was a high school student. My grandfather, Don Regulo, as she called him, was putting her through high school and would later pay for her college. During meals, Orfi and Gladys ate in the kitchen with the maid. This—along with my mother's position as the favorite woman of the household, and the trip to Europe that my grandfather gave her one year—sparked jealousy in them.

I was ten years old when I found a macaw on the roof of the house next door, "la casa de las citas," as my grandfather called it. Every night Colombian women entertained men inside that house. We lived with him on the top floor of a three-story apartment building in Bogotá, and from there we had a view of the roof of the neighbors' house. One day, walking down the hallway, I discovered the bird, standing like a prince, in a crimson feathered cloak. He was large, imposing, his tail majestic. No one knew how this exotic creature had ended up in Bogotá, in our neighborhood, or why it stayed. Where did he come from? Was he lost? How far had the bird flown, and from where—the Amazon? And why was it alone, without a mate, patrolling that roof, calling the women whores? Every time I walked along the long corridor with glass windows on one side, I looked for the bird—pacing, or standing still, observing. Soon, my brother and I started throwing morsels of meat, cereal, and bread on the roof for him to eat. After a few days, we decided to name him George. George became a family member. We were aware of his presence, as he was of ours, though he never came into the house. Often, we tried luring him on a broom stick so we could bring him in, but he refused to climb on that fake branch. Wild and independent, he seemed lost, but like me, he refused to be owned, domesticated.

Saturday nights, when the people next door threw parties, George stood still on the roof. He didn't judge. He just stood, like a Buddhist on his meditation cushion, paying attention, listening to music and shouting as he did when we spoke to him from the open window in the hallway. Now and then, when the women arrived in taxis, George would start pacing, flapping his wings and screaming "Putas!" a word he had learned from my grandfather. When it rained, George sat quietly, raindrops sliding down his feathers, his head down as if in prayer, or looking for worms.

La casa de las citas provided entertainment. We spent evenings at the window watching women wearing tight, short dresses, sequins, high heels, red lips. Some days, a long line of cabs—cream and turquoise, the colors of the Bogotá Hilton—took up the whole street. They waited outside the house long after daybreak, until American and European businessmen, dignitaries, corporate executives, politicians and police officers were ready to leave.

I grew up without a father, but I grew up with a grandfather who loved poetry. From him, I learned Hamlet's soliloquy "To be or not to be…" in Spanish (Ser o no ser), Neruda's "Poema XX" and Alfonsina Storni's "Capricho." He also taught me Lorca, and the meaning of duende (the power to attract, to have magnetism, have soul). Afternoons, he stood by the window listening to me recite poems, helping me remember words, sometimes whole lines. I still recall verses from Ruben Darío's "Sonatina," lines he repeated endlessly, like a mantra. My grandmother found refuge in religion; prayer was her solace. Poetry was Grandfather's prayer.

The year Berta Singerman, an Argentinian actress, performed at The Teatro Colón during her South American tour, Papá Regulo took me to the show. I was eight, but I'll never forget how Singerman recited "Capricho" and other poems by Alfonsina Storni with irony in her voice. I didn't know, then, that at twenty Storni had a child out of wedlock with a married man, and that in 1938, at 46, she jumped into the sea. I didn't know, but my grandfather must have known, while he was teaching me her poems, listening to me repeat her lines. In spite of the traditional roles he seemed to play at home and at work, patriarch, entrepreneur, and ladies man, he could look beyond his personal circumstances and his world, see and understand art and artists, including women artists.

At the age of twelve, I moved to Atlanta with my mother's sister, an aunt I barely knew. Maria, who seldom visited Colombia, had married a man from Alabama. After twelve years in Madrid working for the U.S. government, they had moved to Georgia. I spent a year with her and her family in a suburb of Atlanta, attending seventh grade. I didn't know English, and it was difficult. When summer came, Maria put me on a plane to Wisconsin. She planned to travel to Madrid with her daughter and didn't want to take me, so she had decided I would go stay with my father. I had an address for him—we had exchanged superficial "letters," if I could call them that.

So, my thirteenth summer was spent in a trailer in Sturgeon Bay with my father and his girlfriend, Julie. A month or so after my arrival, my mother and my brother showed up. We all lived with Julie and my father in the trailer until the end of the summer. Soon after the judge established an amount for child support that my father would never honor, and after my parents signed the divorce papers, Grandpapa Regulo sent us tickets so we flew home.

When I was fourteen, my mother moved to Maryland. She took my brother and left me in Bogotá with my uncle Eduardo and his family. My uncle lived in Chapinero, in one of my grandfather's houses, which had a ground floor apartment next door where Mamá Inés and Aunt Lucy, my mother's half-sister, lived. I spent many afternoons with Mamá Inés and Lucy that year, listening to Julio Iglesias's songs, waiting for my mother to send me an airplane ticket. It came in June. Soon after my arrival in Maryland, I got my first job selling chocolates at Fanny Farmer. My Rockville years were spent among chocolate covered cherries and pecan clusters.

It was 1978, the summer of my 17th year to heaven and hell. After signing up for a summer course at the University of Salamanca, I traveled to Europe for the first time. In Spain, I became Esperanza. In love with Salamanca, the countryside, and Spaniards, I decided to take the spring semester off from Montgomery College and return to Salamanca. I convinced my brother to go with me. We passed our days in Spain eating churros con chocolate, dancing at the discotheques, sitting in Plaza Mayor, dreaming of reason, reading *El País*. We had little money and no classes to attend, but we learned to live a sweet life.

WILLIAMSBURG, VIRGINIA, AND HUSBAND NUMBER ONE

If I've ever had any carefree days in my life, besides those in Salamanca, these were spent in Williamsburg. I had never been to that part of Virginia, but after a weekend in Williamsburg with her new husband, my mother returned filled with enthusiasm for the town, the college, its students. William and Mary was affordable too, even for out-of-state students, so I applied, got in, and qualified for student loans. In Williamsburg, for the first time since I had moved to the States, I didn't have to work. No more chocolate covered cherries, boutique clothing, children's section at MEMCO's. I had never seen the campus, or the town—so different from the world in which I grew up. I probably got there a week before classes started. As one of the three Hispanics in the college, I found myself immersed in a soup of sorority girls, fraternity boys, mostly Virginians. I didn't join a sorority, didn't play a sport, I majored in English and minored in History.

John Snyder and I met in 1980, in a French history class. Since I sat in the front row, and he sat in the back, I didn't notice him until I read aloud my paper about Robespierre. He was the only student who listened to what I had to say. He agreed with those who thought Robespierre had been misunderstood throughout history. At least, he nodded while I spoke. When John's turn came to present, he looked mostly at me.

Months later, one evening when someone accidentally hit me on the head with a chair as we sat waiting for Benigno Aquino, the guest speaker, to appear, John asked if I was okay, and if we could have a blond beer after Aquino's speech. Aquino was in the States seeking medical treatment following a heart attack, and he had been invited to William and Mary by a fellow countryman who taught at the college. As John and I sat in the Wigwam drinking beer and commenting on Aquino's moving speech, we didn't know that three years later he would be assassinated.

John was southern gentry, his mother a Daughter of the American Revolution, related to Charles James Faulkner Sr. (1806-1884) who was United States Minister to France when the Civil War began, but in 1861 was recalled to America by Lincoln and later served on Stonewall Jackson's staff. His father's Protestant ancestors came from Bavaria escaping religious persecution. The Snyder family had always lived in Shepherdstown, the oldest town in West Virginia, and they owned and ran *The Shepherdstown Register*, one of the local papers. John's father died when John was studying in Germany his junior year, and he returned to work in the family printing plant in Western Maryland, so he might try to save it from bankruptcy. Due to his father's will, he could not inherit the business until he turned twenty-five or had a college degree, so he went back to William and Mary.

If John was fresh air, kind, and soft, I was earth, water, and rain. I guess that makes mud. He'd grown up in a family in which, for the most part, people stayed married. I had never met a happy couple. His mother, a Pentecostal, wanted him to take care of her, live at home, run the business, certainly not marry a Catholic girl. I was an intruder who didn't belong in their house or their world, a piece from a different puzzle, which would never fit, a "foreigner". From the very beginning, John had to choose between me and his mother. I barely held him for four years, four tumultuous years during which his mother and sister battled him for the business.

I married John, graduated from William and Mary at twenty-one, and enrolled in a Master's program in Spanish literature at George Washington University. Inés Azar, one of my GW professors and a brilliant woman, encouraged me to apply to the Ph.D. program in Spanish at Hopkins, her alma mater. I attended Hopkins during the embattled years, the struggle between John and his family. Having already lived through an inheritance war when my grandfather had died,

I knew no one would win. During my initial interview at Hopkins, the department chair had mentioned the possibility of studying one semester in Florence, if I wanted to learn Italian and work on comparative literature. A year and a half into the program, I decided to go to Florence. I had grown tired of the environment at Hopkins, post-structuralism, the focus on criticism rather than literature, and I had grown very tired of the dangers of living in Baltimore. Evenings, I needed an escort to walk from the library to my efficiency, close by. John was often gone, running the plant in Hagerstown, an hour and a half away. His relationship with his family had worsened, and his frustration grew daily. He was unhappy. By the time I left for Italy, I was running away from my marriage, my husband's family, literary criticism, and John, alas.

FIRENZE AND HUSBAND NUMBER TWO

In Florence, I became Speranza, an exotic woman with an unusual name, for while speranza is not a name, Italians use the word "hope," or "speranza" often. In Tuscany I met Stefano Rossi, a traveling salesman and a Franco Nero look-alike who would become my second husband. He lived in a villa an hour from Florence, with vineyards, and, of course, views of the Tuscan countryside as seen in Italian Renaissance painting. At thirty-three, alone in his large villa, Stefano dined on steak and his family's chianti. At the time, he struck me as a character in a novel by Stendhal. Almost a year earlier, his wife had left him and their two children to move in with another man in Mercatale, three kilometers down the road, and Stefano's parents had taken the children to live with them in Milan. I fell in love with Tuscany, the food, the culture, the language. I thought I was in love with Stefano too.

Stefano was born in Fiesole, the oldest of three children and the Duke Orlandi's grandson, on his mother's side, but he inherited no property due to the laws of primogeniture. His Tuscan parents lived in Milan, where he attended San Carlo, an exclusive *collegio*. Until he got a girl pregnant, Stefano planned to go to law school. Instead, he married her, and took a job selling *commedia dell'arte* doorknobs for the same company as his father. When I met him, he drove all over Tuscany, Emilia Romagna, and Le Marche selling doorknobs, handles and industrial products. He was very successful, and became even more so during our years together. Nine years older than I was, he seemed to understand me better and appreciate me more than John did. John was a *vino novello* when we met. He needed time to mature into a fuller, richer wine. Stefano was a Brunello: dark, rich, filled with flavor. But even the most sophisticated wine connoisseurs grow tired of Brunello if they have to drink it with every meal.

At the beginning, I went with him everywhere. Those first few months were wonderful, perfecting my Italian, getting to know the country. After four years, our daughter, Stephany, was born. Her name ends with a "y" because Stefano (who doesn't speak English) took the opportunity to use this letter, an American touch, in his opinion. We married when Stephany was about two, after Stefano's divorce was finalized.

With time, the understanding that Stefano had initially shown towards me vanished. Perhaps he thought I would forget about completing my Ph.D., being a writer, sculpting. During my pregnancy, I had started taking sculpting lessons in a studio on Via della Pergola, close to the university. Shortly before giving birth I completed a terracotta sculpture of mother and child, so large, it reached up to my knees and I couldn't carry it. My teacher fired it in the oven, and brought it over after Stephany was born. For years, it sat in the floor of my study in Tuscany, close to the fireplace. After I left, Stefano destroyed it.

When I was six months pregnant, to humor me, Stefano agreed to drive to England so I could take a first look at British universities. The trip across the channel from Calais to Dover was long, the ferry ride very unpleasant. The people at Oxford and Cambridge barely looked at me, indifferent to my interest in their Ph.D. programs. At the University of Manchester, Jeremy Laurence, an Oxford graduate, listened intently as I told him that I lived in Italy with the Italian man standing behind me, and wanted to complete my Ph.D. in Manchester. "I think you'll be able to start in two years," he said, "get in touch with me then." And so, I did. Stefano probably thought that after having a child I would give up on Manchester, would never complete my dissertation. As a U.S. citizen, my tuition would cost thousands of pounds. When Jeremy petitioned the university so I could register as a European student, paying 400 pounds a year, Stefano could not argue that it was too expensive.

At a bus stop in front of the Biblioteca Marucelliana in Florence I met Sergio Bertelli, the chair of the history department at the university. He had a stack of books he was taking to his studio at Bellosguardo, located close to Porta Romana, and to the apartment where I lived with Stefano and Stephany. I felt isolated living in the villa close to Mercatale, and had convinced Stefano to rent a place in Florence. Bertelli and I exchanged numbers, and agreed that I would go see him at the university. He was familiar with the subject of my dissertation, Alfonso V of Aragon and his royal entries into Naples during the XV century, and offered to help me during a crucial time when I was lonely, far away from Manchester and from my thesis supervisor, trying to figure out an original approach. Although I wrote about entries, exits turned out to be my area of expertise: exiting marriages, countries, jobs.

After I started working with Bertelli, Stefano became insanely jealous. Even though this was not the first time he acted jealous, his temper tantrums grew more frequent; nights when he indulged in one of his tirades, he attacked those "intellettuali di merda"—referring to Bertelli and his circle, which included me, of course. When he started following me around Florence, our fights got worse. Without any money, without a job, with a partially completed degree in literature, and a daughter, my choices were few. I had left the U.S. saying I would never return. Unlike George the macaw, I had stepped on the broom stick Stefano had offered me. I had gone into his house, and was living under a borrowed roof. Now, I didn't know how to leave. But I had abandoned my Ph.D. program and my fellowship at Hopkins, and I had to complete that degree. My determination to complete the Ph.D. kept me in Europe longer than I would have stayed. My daughter's future gave me the impetus to leave. I didn't want her to grow up watching her parents fight, witnessing an unhappy marriage.

I spent four years traveling between Florence and Manchester, years researching in libraries in Rome, Florence, Naples, London, years writing, meeting with Jeremy, working with Bertelli. Having had only one semester of Latin at Hopkins, I had to teach myself. Many of the documents were in Catalan or in Neapolitan dialect. I had to learn those as well.

A month after my orals in Manchester, I left Italy under the pretext that I would be visiting my mother. I bought two one way tickets, and took only one suitcase. If Stefano found out that I was leaving him, he would try to take Stephany away from me, to punish me. When he was sure that I would not go back despite all his pleading, he put out a warrant for my arrest, and accused me of stealing not only my daughter, but also his family jewels. If I had taken them, I would not have given them up for a wilderness of monkeys.

After leaving Stefano, I came back to the DC area and called George Washington University to inquire about teaching positions. They were short on teachers, and offered me four courses each semester for a year. An adjunct's salary is not much, but it was more than what I had in Italy. A few months later, I moved from my mother's house to a furnished efficiency, and I enrolled Stephany in Our Lady of Lourdes, nearby. I did the best I could as a single mother, taking my daughter to a school where they didn't speak Italian, going to work, picking her up from after-school care. I had practically raised her alone as Stefano continued to build his door knob selling career, but now I was my own and my child's bread winner.

SHEPHERDSTOWN AND HUSBAND NUMBER THREE

During my Italian years and after our divorce, John and I remained friends. We sent Christmas cards, exchanged phone calls. While I was gone, he lived with two different women, and almost married one. He printed the invitations, but just before they were mailed, he called the wedding off. During my absence, he had time to work things out with his family, and to turn the printing company around.

John and I started seeing each other again while I was living at the Topaz House and teaching at GW. He had always wanted children, and he and Stephany got along. One day, when I had to teach and couldn't make it to a school show, John offered to go for me. At the end of the show, when children went up to their parents, my six-year-old daughter ran into his arms.

While at GW, I looked for a full-time teaching position. I had several interviews, but, ironically, the best job offer came from Shepherd University, in Shepherdstown, West Virginia, John's hometown. I took the job, and moved nearby. Once my divorce from Stefano came through in 1998 John and I re-married. It was a year after our son, William, was born. This time, we married in the Wren Chapel at William and Mary, where we first met. Our second wedding was at the end of March, seventeen years and one month after our first wedding. I wore white, of course. Since then, we've had another child, and named her Isabella Inés, after my grandmother.

Born in a bathtub filled with water, Esperanza Snyder grew up first as Sister, then as Lee. In Rockville, Maryland, she became Hope Carey Maxwell, the name stamped on her passport. In Salamanca, her name was Esperanza. No one cared about her last name. When she married John Wiltshire Snyder, a fourth-generation printer, she became Hope Maxwell Snyder. In a moment of anger towards her father, she started using Hope Carey Snyder, but that didn't last long. During her years in Florence she became Speranza. Once again, no one cared about her last name. After meeting Stefano and divorcing John, she hadn't changed her name. It was still Hope Maxwell Snyder on her passport. In Florence, she published several articles about Alfonso V of Aragon, and Sergio Bertelli, the co-author of one of the articles, said she should use Hope Maxwell, which she did. She married Stefano Rossi (whose mother was an Orlandi, related to the Pazzi family in Florence) but she never took his last name. Too much paperwork. Plus, he enjoyed having "an American wife." In Manchester, Esperanza was Hope, and signed her dissertation Hope Maxwell. After permanently returning to the U.S. nine years later, she kept Hope Maxwell Snyder, which worked very well when she and John married for the second time. But now, after all these years, after three husbands, three children, four imperfect languages, many jobs, she's realized that she is, and always was, Esperanza. Esperanza Snyder. Names, after all, are about family history, love, love of country, love of language.

COLOMBIA

MY FATHER'S LETTER

On my knees, I studied the light, Neruda-blue envelope
with red and blue stripes, stamped with American words,
messy handwriting. We found it in the post office box
downtown. In her short skirt (refusing to bend)
my mother handed me the key. At the gold Museum
across the street, people stood in line. For twenty pesos
they walked into a dark room and waited for light
to shine on masks, decanters, 24 karat bracelets,
rafts re-telling the story of El Dorado, gold
forgotten in forgotten trunks meant for Malaga.
In front of the museum leaves shivering on trees
announced impending storms. Food vendors sold
hot dogs and empanadas. My mother tore the envelope.
His letter, as brief as a butterfly's hours, scribbled
with words I didn't understand. The sheet of onionskin
trembled in my mother's hands. She read in silence,
in a hurry, before taking lipstick from her purse,
a mirror, and painting her lips red. Then, she
tore the letter up. In silence, without stopping
to catch our breath, we waited for the bus.
I held the letter in my hand, half full of hate.
I could not remember his hand holding mine
with a touch of love. The pain of my life, searching
for my father's love without hope, esperanza.

MY FATHER'S LANGUAGE

He doesn't understand the texture of papaya,
double rs, or the difference between *ser* and *estar*.
Women's thighs confuse him. He drills students,
chews gum, drinks maple syrup in the bathtub.
From the hotel window his voice whistles by palm
trees, stirring centurial dust that sticks to skin.
Women pay to stare at his tailored shirts, hay hair,
lips, swollen or full. Mascara, caked into clouds,
predicts future storms. Mamá soaks in fountains, rubs
her breasts with Neroli oil. They married in Alabama,
during her year abroad, a semester of grits, beauty
contests, Venezuelan men. Father doesn't understand
my mother's rage, her pride, her morning scowls. Most
nights, it's impossible to breathe, impossible to share
the small room, what's left of the money. I pass beggars
on the street, look the other way. Most mornings he refuses
to get up for class. It won't last, Mamá's faith in him,
his love for her. She lies on the sofa naked, almost absent.

BLUE NIGHTS

Neruda's color was blue, sky blue, dark blue
like the color of the night, blue
like the sweater rolled under his feet,
blue like a hurt dog, blue like a silent blue shore,
and blue like the ocean, sometimes sinister
and endless, sometimes crystalline,
turquoise, the sand on the bottom clean
as a blank sheet. Like the poet, the ocean
always changes. Even his name,
taken from Jan Neruda who lived and wrote
in Prague where there is a street named after him,
though when tourists see it they think of Pablo,
because at the age of twenty he wrote:
"Tonight, I can write the saddest lines.
Write, for instance: the night is starred,
and blue stars tremble in the distance."
At nine, I knew this poem by heart and stood
in a sala in Bogotá reciting it for my grandfather
who loved to hear it after work. We lived
with him, and he taught me to repeat,
remember, enunciate, where to pause,
what syllables to stress. Evenings before dinner,
I recited the poem without paying attention
to the words, except what followed what,
never wondering if my grandfather shared
Neruda's longing, never thinking
of a woman who lived somewhere else
in the city and looked too worn out for love,
nor the woman who shared Grandfather's
bed and looked too fat for love. But
my grandfather gave me Neruda's music,

and Neruda gave me blue nights, blue,
blue, blue, and the words to describe
your body, how it tastes of wine and apples.

PHOTOGRAPH OF A MAN
STANDING BY A WATERFALL

This is the only picture of our father.
He's holding my brother like a cherub in a Florentine painting.
Papá, no longer just a voice over the telephone
long distance from *los Estados Unidos,*
or a writer of impersonal letters
who includes self-addressed, stamped envelopes
for our replies about our lives without him.
Nude torso, the waterfall behind him, bamboo, palms,
large slabs of rock, this place a circus and a carnival at once,
a land of heat and evergreens I don't know.
Strong as a centaur, white without apology, in the picture
our father wears tight bathing trunks,
his blond hair already an M on his forehead.
Thick lips, no smile, cleft chin, a body made for love
and betrayal, made for running away.

OUT OF THE BLUE

On foggy mornings I sit on mother's bed.
She braids my hair, grinds her teeth.
Outside, the school bus waits. The driver honks.
On the way home, Maria Fernanda will undo
my mother's work. She is taller,
her obsidian hair twisted into a bun.
Horse's teeth shine when she laughs.
If I sit by the other Maria Fernanda, the one
with high cheek bones and a uniform skirt so short
she cannot bend, out of the blue, we draw dolls.
Her long wavy hair dances when she walks.
On Saturdays, Aunt Lucy sprinkles beer in my hair
before braiding, to help it grow. I'm told
she had thick braids before her foolish
mess, her son. They all play mothers
with me now our fathers are gone.

CHILDHOOD COMPANION

I think of us, and other children, wrapped
in blankets, speeding by pastures, mountains,
the air cooling as we reached Bogotá
in the back of the Mercury pickup.
For years, this was my only memory of her,
this, and looking at the darkened country sky at night
listening to her stories about *La Llorona*.
Hearing the words of this lame girl, our leader,
older than us, bitter beyond her years,
we trembled, went to bed praying,
hoping to hold it in 'til dawn, so *la Llorona*
couldn't chase us into a bathroom
of bats flying in through glassless windows.
No one knew her father. She never mentioned
him. She must've gotten pleasure
out of scaring us, her payback for not sitting
at the dinner table, but in the kitchen,
with her mother, who planned and cooked
our meals, and, after dark, went to my grandfather.

LECHE

We stand outside. Gladys holds my hand.
I stare at plastic bags forgotten
on the front steps of our flat, *La Lechera*
scribbled in blue across the front.
I don't know why milk spoiling in the sunlight
makes me sad. From her, I learned
—too soon—how girls turn into women.
Her fat mother orders silk dresses
from China, drags her large body around,
cooking, dusting, cleaning, and, at bedtime,
to my grandfather. One leg shorter
than the other, Gladys and her shoes
echo in the hallways. She's always mad,
always studying Geometry, always flunking.
One day, I'll know Geometry investigates
properties, relations of magnitudes in space,
lines, surfaces, solids. One day, I'll know
Gladys in Latin means lame. In her room,
in the back of the flat, I learned—too soon—
about love from her stone-cold hands.
Her room, next to the maid's quarters,
next to the outdoor sink dripping water.
Oh, if I could stroke the surface of a circle,
learn its shape, dream a world, of perfect
symmetry, and safe. Oh, if I could
accept my body's shape, and my heart's,
but what sort of broken shape is that?

GLADYS

Older than the rest of us, Gladys has her own room
in the back. Her father, an absent tailor, sews invisible
clothes. Grandfather's putting her through school.
He sighs when she walks in the room.
A round flat face, Asian-looking eyes, a voice
so shrill, we pray she doesn't talk.
The bitterness she spreads around the flat covers us in dust.
She wears a blackness that I wish I'd never touched,
but Gladys wants to hold my hand, go for walks,
tell me about men and what they do to us.
She explains how babies are born, in a monotone,
as if she knew, as if there were no miracles involved.

IRONING LESSONS

My poem is about memories of women
ironing in Bogotá—my aunt,
my grandmother, the maid,
the woman sleeping in Grandfather's bed,
and about the time I tried to learn
and burned my elbow and my hand,
and how these scars have been with me since then,
with other wounds, more subtle, impossible to judge.
Who taught me? Someone who didn't mind seeing me
hurt. Perhaps the maid, the woman
sleeping in Grandfather's bed, or her daughter,
always teaching me dangerous games.

MY GRANDFATHER, 1910-1982

He died when I was overseas building a life, working.
His picture, on my desk, to me, he never died.
I didn't make it to his funeral, never visited his grave,
yet all the poems I learned from him remain fragmented in me.

Teatro Colón. How small the stage now seems, how empty
the velvet seats, how far away the front row,
faded chandelier, dull wood floor where Berta Singerman
stood that night—diaphanous blouse, red hair, scarf.

My grandfather stood at the window of his place for years
in Bogotá, studying the world, smoking *Piel Roja* cigarettes.
One hand in the pocket of his trousers, a cigarette in the other,
he'd whisper Alfonsina's words. She took her life in 1938.

My grandfather loved women but didn't know *how* to love them.
Living apart from my grandmother, another woman in his bed,
he loved Alfonsina and her words, like he loved
Singerman, the way she repeated Alfonsina's lines.

All those times I recited "Capricho" for my grandfather,
I didn't know this poem he loved, lines he longed to hear
me say, were written by a woman who jumped into the sea
forever. *The sea we carry sea inside often floods our eyes.*

Men found Alfonsina's drowned body, then stood,
smoking on the beach, talking. They stared at her naked back,
her hair, tangled with seaweed. It was that hour
between night and day, closer to dawn than darkness.

The year Berta Singerman performed "Capricho" at the Colón,
poetry was born for me. The actress spoke to an absent lover,
on an empty stage, laughing, explaining away her sadness.
Don't ask me why I cried so much last night.

All these years, carrying lines of this poem inside me,
lines learned from Singerman and from Papá.
I thought it was for fun—to make Papá Regulo laugh—
that I stood in the middle of the sala in Bogotá, reciting.

I was too young to understand that love
can drive you mad. Now, I sense a touch of madness
in Alfonsina's words, madness in Singerman's laughter
when she said them, madness in my grandfather.

THE WAY THINGS WERE

Here's how it was: the two of us, and mother,
in a room with room enough for three beds
living with other strays like us—in that crowded
flat—while father found a new life over the seas.
The way things were, we tiptoed around her anger,
looked out for each other, learned to read
her weather, turned quiet like stones, invisible
like wind, during her thunderstorms.
I learned to toss my report card—splashed
in red—on the bed for her to sign,
before running off to take the school bus
honking outside. It wasn't that I wasn't smart,
or grateful, when she yelled, again, that her job
at Sacred Heart paid for our school.
It's just that those red marks were
the only voice I had, my bloody anger.
The way things were, we never cried, but tried
to be adults. We never called her Mother,
only by her first name, as we were told. At parties,
we were siblings, *los hermanitos* Maxwell.
For hours—often until dawn—she danced,
pretending she was free, forgetting we were hers.
I don't blame her for wanting more.
She was young, her long hair, obsidian black.

TRAVELING WITH MY BROTHER
TO SEE POPE JOHN PAUL

Dressed for church, holding hands, we follow
crowds, take a Volkswagen bus, lose ourselves
in the warm breath of strangers lingering too close
to us under the midday sun, *campesinos* wearing
ponchos, women in high heels, their small hands,
warm inside white gloves, digging inside purses
full of pesos, priests in starched collars, nuns
counting beads, praying to John Paul, praying
for world peace, etcetera. Our instructions,
to stay close to a woman so fat, we can't lose her,
her red dress, her daughter. At nine and seven
all this faith could knock us over, but we knew
what we desired, we knew what to pray for.
Our first train ride, velvet cushions—pink
as the Virgin's tongue—cushion our journey
to the stadium where His Holiness will arrive
in white robes, standing in a Jeep like a Sandinista.
For the Pope's benediction, the fat woman
will get on her knees, tear her sins away,
lift one arm to catch more blessings. Incense
fills our lungs, empties our bellies, makes us
swoon. On our knees, we pray for *ajiaco*, pray
for Sara, our mother, in Madrid. Soon,
she'll be home, with a blue suede miniskirt,
chocolates, and a new way of naming things,
fancying herself an *Infanta*, pronouncing
azul like a Spaniard, tongue behind teeth.

TAKING CARE OF THINGS

She remembers the school by a lake,
and remembers staying outside
until the bus driver turned on the engine,
honked, though she doesn't remember
exactly what games she played,
just as she doesn't remember the day
her brother and his friends hid bees
inside her desk. She doesn't remember
getting stung, but she sees bees
getting caught in her teacher's
blonde-white bun. Now she knows
it's called a beehive, that hairstyle,
and she understands why the teacher wept.
After the buses left,
in caravan, she sat at a window seat,
in the back, for the two hours home.
She doesn't remember her mother's anger
at seeing the tire tracks on her flat lunchbox,
but she remembers Sara saying,
"you don't take care of things."
Like the Swiss watch. Like
the doll she boiled in soap. Like
the double-breasted Spanish pink coat.
"Palo de Rosa" was what her mother called
that particular shade of pink.
Too warm for her climate, it hung
in the closet until she outgrew it.

THE YEAR I LIVE WITH MY COUSIN

She shortens her uniform skirt and during recess at *Sagrado Corazón* drinks *aguardiente* and coke she brings from home.

At sixteen, she has a woman's body, wide hips, a short frame she carries on platform shoes, clunky like Geisha sandals.

This is the year of our first boyfriends, the Mustafa brothers, Palestinian exiles studying Spanish in college.

This is the year before I leave for Maryland to meet my brother and mother, the year before my cousin becomes a mother.

Using a safety pin, she traces the shape of a heart on her wrist over and over again, until blood stains her blouse.

"This is how you do it" she tells me, licking her skin, wiping the stain with a tissue. "It hurts, but you get used to it."

MAMÁ INÉS

She walked slowly with a cane, like a seagull on the sand,
never saw the ocean, never left our land,
didn't learn to swim, or taste salt water on her tongue.

She lit candles, one by one, in a small room in the back,
like a priestess in her chapel, like a female
Hephaestus, bent and crippled, matches trembling in her hand.
First, the spark, then, the flame, white and wild, green, red
as Grandmother, in her shawl, knelt before Jesus,
before god, rosary trembling in her hands.

Lighting burners on the stove, making sweet *café con leche*,
serving soft bread from the bakery next door, she was always
serving us, time slipping away. What was left, went to Achilles.

LORCA AND MY GRANDFATHER

The day they died, large stars of frost came
with the fish of shadows to open the way for dawn.
They left three-piece suits in their closets,
hand-made hats on the shelves, books of poems.
Con la sombra en la cintura ella sueña en su baranda.
Green are the words in my grandfather's mouth,
green his emeralds, green the veranda in his house.
He put his fingers in his vest pocket, unfolded
paper squares and triangles for emeralds,
green like mountains. *Verde que te quiero verde.*
Verde viento. Verdes ramas. Blue, my father's eyes,
white his lipstick-stained shirt, drying
on the clothesline. Green, my mother's jealousy,
red her anger. She leans on the green veranda
counting bells as they chime. *Verde carne, pelo verde,*
ojos de fría plata. Sunday mornings she kisses
a worn-down crucifix by her bed, scrambles eggs
with her fingers, refuses to go to church.
Green is her new found sadness that tastes
of copper and dirt, green her words,
like Lorca's branches, green the lady of death.
Bajo la luna gitana/las cosas le están mirando
y ella no puede mirarlas. Now they're gone,
my country is no longer my country, my house
no longer my house. I look for them in the branches,
green with sadness. Alone on the green veranda
since I was a child. How long I waited for them,
clean face, green hair. How long I waited—crying—
with sugar cubes in my mouth. This country is no longer
my country. This house is no longer my house. Verdes.
Los quería verdes. Verde esmeralda, verde esperanza.

ELEGY FOR MY GRANDFATHER
WHO LIVED IN A CITY SURROUNDED
BY MOUNTAINS

He was light reflected on snow,
a handful of emeralds in the mouth,
high cheekbones shaped as *Chibcha*
clouds. He was rain, a hotel room
in Vallejo's Paris, legs that walked
through wilderness for miles.
Soft and hard like the seed
of the *mamoncillo* fruit
covered in bitter-sweet pulp.
Long after his body forgot
to speak the language of desire
poems bloomed under his hat.
In his room, a window, brandy,
Neruda, candles, and Daedalus's
wings, traded for a pound of coffee
in Damascus. The year he watched
the world from his bed, I danced
flamenco for him. In those days,
I was still a spider, all arms and legs,
all making threads for webs.

MAR DEL PLATA, WHERE ALFONSINA WALKED INTO THE SEA

Then it was dawn. And in those first rays
of light and life and wave her body
floated back to shore, the place
from which she'd come, leaving
her hotel room after midnight, after
sealing her last poem in an envelope,
barefoot, in a skirt and camisole that later
she would strip off under the moonlight
before stepping into the water, before
walking away, before trying not to think
of her son, his face after he read her letter.
At that hour the temperature was cool,
the water cobalt and colder, her skin
all goose bumps, her heart working
to keep her warm. She would walk,
she wrote, to the bottom of the sea,
to a glass house she built at the end
of a white coral street. When her feet
touched the water, she was frightened,
I think, because the darkness and the cold,
and her nakedness, felt wrong. She
straightened her back, lowered her arms,
raised her chin, looked straight into
the darkness. Later, too late to change
her mind, she swallowed the Atlantic.
For a moment, my lungs fill with water,
like hers, sea sponges in the rain.

CONFESSIONS FOR THE GUERRILLA
FIGHTER UPSTAIRS

The street, empty of your bodyguards,
empty your house, empty the Chivas bottle,
empty my bed, empty our dawn. Your army
uniform hangs empty in the vacant closet
in my home. Your t-shirt and my blouse on the
laundry line like freshly laundered peace flags.
I scribbled graffiti on your door. I was drunk,
tired of hearing your speeches to the press,
news of money you took from enemies
and friends, your pretty girls, your libido,
the sex. For me, it was always our cheeks,
rosy after love, your hands, clean in the light,
clean on my skin, your bloodless nails.
I heard of your boots on mountain trails,
of your men and women burning farms,
taking children from their homes to teach
them, not how to read, but how to load a rifle.
I water plants, clip dead leaves off
stems, buy black negligees, wear crimson
lipstick, sweep tiles, dream your airplane
stark and desolate in the clouds, my lips
moist with wine, moist with you.

INGRID BETANCOURT SPEAKS
AFTER HER RELEASE

That is the hammock. Those are the poles it hung from.
That is the net I kept over my head. That is the chain
they wrapped around my ankle. The tree I was bound to.
This is my Bible. Those are mangoes I ate when I was starving.
That is my box. These are my children in the photograph,
six years younger. These scars are scorpion bites.
That naked man on the floor, blindfolded, was my captor.
This is my rosary. I made it with buttons from the shirts,
skirts, pants and jackets of victims. My fingers count:
for each button a victim, for each victim, a prayer.

WHAT I REMEMBER ABOUT
MY BROTHER'S FIRST WEDDING IS…

Drinking to love, casting an empty *aguardiente* bottle
into the old lake Guatavita, not the new one,
with its church steeple rising above the waters.
Hearing planes at night mistaking the lake for a runway,
down, like the old town, waiting under water,
with its empty houses, its experimental sorrows.
And I remember riding back to Bogotá in silence,
like the time he rode back home to find the door locked,
his clothes piled up outside, another man behind its walls.

NERUDA WROTE TWENTY LOVE POEMS

and a desperate song. My grandfather learned Neruda's
words by heart, so he could say them in the mornings
after coffee, and evenings, standing by the window

watching *extranjeros* arrive next door for parties,
women, whisky, empanadas, love, before
leaving early morning in their Hilton taxis to fly home.

We were all a little broken then, all a little lost,
like lost sailboats: My mother and her broken marriage,
her suitors, and her angers, my father, god knows where,

my grandmother across town, praying for her daily bread,
the fat woman in Grandfather's bed, rising early, baking
bread, bickering with Mother, bickering with the maid,

and the children, all of us, all our lives, eating the maid's
finger-scrambled eggs, so she wouldn't lose her job.
And the lies, O, the lies.

EUROPA

MEMORY IN THE WINE

This trip. This seat. This wine. This bottle. This wine.
This sleep. This empty heart. This love, quickly crawling,
light floating outside the window of the plane. This silence.
This glass. This trembling. That is where I lie on the bed
by the wall, next to a window in the first light. How
soon, how well, should a man and a woman make love?
How soon, how well, have I loved? On the bed, on the couch,
on the couch, on the bed. Love, in a train wreck, love, like
a cold bath. Love, like a brimming purse and a brimming
purse heavy and overpowering. This trip. This seat. This wine,
this torture. This book. This poem in a book. This wine
on the tongue. This memory in the wine.

SALAMANCA

Early summer mornings I watch the light fall
on the stone balconies in Plaza Mayor.
Evenings I follow couples walking around the Plaza
arm in arm, and eavesdrop, in love with their names
for the world, *azul, corazón, zapato,* young Goya.
Six months later, after our mother's new husband
says it won't work for us to stay, I return to Salamanca
and bring my brother with me. We sit on benches
in the old cathedral, stand by the altar in the new one,
delicately built, like lace, remembering our grandfather
and his favorite Unamuno novel, *Niebla,*
in which a dog named Orpheus delivers a speech
at his master's grave. I see our grandfather
in the old men of Salamanca, same black vest,
same white shirt, same hat, same
skinny dark face, like Unamuno's.

Once a month we cross Plaza Mayor,
walk up a side street to the Western Union
to collect our mother' wire. We have little
money and spend it dancing in Disco Number One,
drinking vodka and Fanta, stopping for *chocolate
con churros* on our way home at dawn,
mist rising from the Duero. Mornings
we linger at Café Novelty reading *El Pais,*
drinking café con leche, watching the sun
warm balconies in Plaza Mayor. This makes it
easier to accept we have no home at "home."

Last week, on a train to Lisbon, my brother made love
to a girl who is getting married in the fall.
Listen, we are both a little lonely, both a little

confused. But listen, here's the point:
at nineteen, I'm still a virgin. This worries me,
like the Spanish *Dons* and *caballeros*, their probing
eyes, the way they look at me. My brother says
I should wait to find someone I can love,
and that love-making is more meaningful that way.
Soon, we'll go to Belgrade for three weeks
to visit Petra, my brother's high school friend.

CANTE FLAMENCO

He kissed me on a cool summer night,
with wine and cinnamon lips.
He kissed the moonlight of my face,
under a million stars, eyes closed,
heart open to dreams.
Nights like these, I dream he takes my hand.
We run up the hill to our church,
and fly like kites at dawn,
white shirts floating over
the fields where Federico died.
In men's hungry eyes, thoughts, clear
as graffiti on church walls.
They want to touch my skin,
but I long to dance only for him,
raise my arms, hide my castanets
in my hands, let them speak.
My dress, sea waves crowned in foam,
ruffles rising, falling, floating polka dots.
La luna studies her face
in the mirror of the sea,
fish open their eyes when my castanets sing.
The day he left, I buried my hunger
in a cave above Granada.
If he returns, my bed will freeze.
The olive trees will burn.
The moon will comb her hair again,
and I will dance for him.
I choose a blue dress
now he's gone, red shoes,
and, like a jaguar, crouch on the edge
of Castille to wait for him.

FALLING

Months in Europe with my brother,
without studying, without work.
We'd left our part-time jobs, our schools,
our mother, to board trains for Paris,
Rome, Belgrade, knowing nothing about war,
nothing about God, or love, art's fluent language.
Nothing about heartbreak. In Madrid,
we drank coffee spiked with cognac, walked
around Plaza Mayor, sat in restaurants for hours.
We had gray days—like the day we saw Picasso's
painting of Guernica— and we had dark,
star-less nights, reminiscent of the night
bombs fell on that Basque town while children
and their parents slept, in April, almost May,
spring outside their windows, wine bottles
forgotten on the tables. And there were cold
days too, like the day at El Retiro Park
when we stood looking at Bellver's angel,
mouth wide open, bronze wings extended,
face facing heaven. Today, I've come
to see the angel, and to remember
that winter day, how my brother looked
in his suede jacket, how soft my face appears
in the photograph, long hair braided to one side.
It's spring, and white, yellow, pink,
red roses bloom under the sun warming
students sunbathing on the grass. Deaf, dumb,
and blind about our days in Spain, except
the way my brother shivered in a light jacket.

TITO'S GONE

We came to this language and this country with a plan
and a fixed number of days. We came to work,
pay our bills, travel a little bit. Like the time
we went to visit Petra in Yugoslavia when Yugoslavia
was still Yugoslavia and Tito was still alive.
Petra was my brother's friend. For three weeks
in Belgrade, at a four-star hotel we couldn't
afford, we ate fresh rolls with butter and jam
while waiting for Petra to pick us up.
In Belgrade we were always waiting, waiting
to visit museums, parks, bars, restaurants,
humble homes. Waiting to hear about Tito's health.
Afternoons, we sat at outdoor cafes by the Danube
drinking coffee spiked with slivovitz,
watching boats dance on the water. It was spring,
roses everywhere: reds, whites, blues, yellows.
It was May, and we were always drunk with music,
beer, and brandy, throwing our days away fast,
like Ferraris on the Autostrada between Modena
and Bologna. I don't know what ghosts my brother
was leaving behind, but I longed to forget Salamanca,
and a man. For months, every night I'd walked
to his house for new lessons, my tutor in heartbreak.
By the end, we sat in Plaza Mayor drinking rum
and coke, staring into space. If he'd wanted me,
I would've stayed with him rather than going
with my brother to Belgrade. It was May,
and we didn't know what to do, how
to behave. Petra and my brother found girls,
and I stayed with Jiri, Petra's friend from Montenegro,
a colonel's son with lips like wedges of grapefruit.
Late at night, in my hotel room, we sat by the radio

waiting to hear news about Tito, listening
to American songs. I tried to teach Jiri
what I'd learned in Spain, but we were too tired
and too drunk to make it work, like Serbia
and Montenegro. On the morning my brother and I
left Belgrade, we were late for the train.
Then, for hours we sat staring out the window
at soldiers in boots and long coats inspecting
our suitcases, studying our passports.
We said goodbye to friends, roses,
the Danube, a country that would soon
dissolve, like Tito, like love.

SUMMER IN MADRID

And now the sunlight, seeping even under the trees,
the unbearable July heat that drives children and mothers
to Malaga, reaches me under the magnolia tree
where I have placed the towel he brought for me,
a cotton cloth sprinkled with stars, smelling
of delicate detergent, and feeling soft under my skin,
my sunburned shoulders. There's not much shade
in this crowded university pool, students
everywhere: on the grass, on the tiles
next to the pool, under the trees, sitting at tables
by the pool, umbrellas opened, standing at the outdoor
bar where music from a radio blends with conversation,
shouts, people drinking, smoking, laughing in this moment,
when somewhere else in Madrid someone is taking a siesta,
someone is taking a train, someone is shutting a door,
and tourists walk down Paseo Recoletos towards El Prado,
suffering the unbearable heat, feet swollen. And now
I'm thinking of my days in Salamanca, the bullfighter's son,
a trip to Sevilla. I've lost his name, but I can see still
see him, too tall to be a matador like his father,
but handsome, strong, with his mother's sweet Peruvian
eyes, a mixed-blood like me, mixed race, mixed heart.
It could be him sunbathing next to me now,
under the magnolia tree, or Chema, the disc jockey
who fell in love with me and played my favorite songs,
or Paco, who owned Maria Sangrienta, a discotheque,
and invited me to London to buy albums, instead
of this rake, this man, from Valladolid, my teacher
in lovemaking and heartbreak. In Salamanca,
when I saw him with another of his women,
how my heart would fly out of me, not like a bird
or a butterfly, but like a goat. And now, not one leaf

is moving, and the clouds don't move. The students
who have come here to swim and play remind me
of our Salamanca winter nights when I believed
he loved me. Now, looking at him on the blanket,
smoking a cigarette next to me, I wonder what it was
that made my heart beat fast when I saw him.

SALAMANCA, SUMMER SUNDAYS

If you cross the bridge from the Parador
into the old part of the city
early in the morning before the day heats up
and the light turns ochre and heavy,
early—when church bells call families to Jesus—
you'll see runners, students on bikes,
doves pecking while the streets are being swept,
and you'll notice hundreds of brass locks
—with dates and names written on them—
hanging from both sides of the railing in clusters
the way grapes hang in the vineyards. To study
the thickness of the black ink used to write
the lovers' names, to read the date each lock
was fastened to the bridge, you must be
on your knees. Numbers give us comfort,
so we measure: date of birth, age, year we met,
year we married, years together, enough equations
for a lifetime. Even death has its own date.
Looking at the locks, I try to guess where
their owners are, if the keys were tossed into El Duero
and lay forgotten there, like my memories of you
and our days in Salamanca. Brass—in the early
morning light—shines like gold on wedding bands.
If you stop halfway down the bridge and turn
around, to your left you'll see canoes resting
by the shore and a white sheet hanging
from two trees: "Juan y Maria se casan,"
Juan and Maria are getting married.
On one side of the sheet, a large heart painted
in black ink with a thick brush. Underneath,
two wooden boats, tied together and waiting.

JULY IN PLAZA SANTA ANA, MADRID

I remember sunrise most, the blue and red glass
in my bedroom, in the hot apartment,
church bells, and owls sounding deep into the night,
choral Beethoven blasting from the open windows
of the half-deaf seamstress's flat two floors below,
before the daily news, and after, a parrot
begging in Spanish for tortilla, and the heat,
hot summer afternoons with *vino tinto de verano*
in the plaza, and bronze Lorca standing,
not in the center of the square,
but to one side, a nightingale in his hands.
Like the statue, I'm lost this far away
from orange groves and rivers, this far away
from home. Wings extended, hot to my touch,
the bird is ready to fly. In the stone square,
early morning before Lorca's tie and coat
take on a bronzed patina, before the *pajarito*
in his hands discovers it will never take off,
when waiters in white shirts and black pants sweep
the pavement, shoo the pigeons off, I sit at Ana's café
watching the light bring murder upon the plaza.
I need silence to understand years spent holding others
the way Lorca holds this bird in his cupped hands,
as if he would set me free at any moment. As if he could.

LIFE IN MERCATALE WITH
MY FUTURE SECOND HUSBAND

No one notices the swelling of my belly
until summer when I shed my clothes
and dive into the pool
in last year's red bikini.
August, the grapes heavy on the vines,
the scent of wine in the air since dawn.
Near the barn, Stefano's two uncles
sharpen their tools,
choose pigs for slaughter.
His mother says she's glad,
that any child of *his* is welcome.
No one mentions his ex-wife,
her long silences over the phone,
the way she drags my laundry
through the mud at night,
the fact that births go wrong.
His uncles watch me walk the field
of sunflowers alone. They watch
stalks sway and close behind me,
my dress a speck of gold.

TWELVE TUSCAN NIGHTS

Without wings we don't fly

I spend most days in my room
looking at books in other languages.
On the twelfth night, Stefano
gets home. He climbs the stairs,
opens the window, smokes a cigarette,
looks at the vineyards. Late
summer, the scent of grapes rises
to my study, sweetness, a little
bitterness, followed by dry earth,
and, not far away, the olive trees,
leaves silver against the sun.
These grapes, these olives,
and this wine, the wine,
fill me with pleasure,
then courage. Summer nights,
the aroma of a garden, basil rising,
frogs by the lake. On nights
like these, it's hard to fall asleep,
hard to find the vineyards
soothing. Come fall,
windows open to dawn
and foggy mountains,
oceans of white, red grapes.
The aroma of espresso
rises from the kitchen.
Outside, hunters shooting birds
smaller than my hands.
I wear my brother's clothes.
No one understands
the indifference of this place,

how slow the hours pass
while I wait, how the days
follow one another, and the nights,
and the seasons. I'm trying to let it all go,
before it swallows me, before
I drown, because music is the food of love.

ARRANGING FLOWERS

Today my friend Keiko will wake early
and walk to Piazza Signoria searching
for color, texture, shape, enough flowers,
branches and leaves for the women.
She will fill her two large canvas bags
with orchids and irises, and she'll carry
the bags back to her flat, where
for hours she'll sit by the open window
in front of her dining room table,
trimming, cutting, shaping nature
the way painters paint. What's left
of the morning she'll spend on her
flowers, her display, Palazzo Pitti
so close she imagines a bridge
of biscotti she'd cross in less
than a minute—she'd run—
and remembers her Ikebana Master
in Japan. As a young girl, she learned
the way of the tea and the way
of the flowers, how to sew a kimono
by hand, how to cook, line
her eyelids, paint her lips red.
How to please, how to marry.
In Firenze, on their way
to Keiko's class, the women
enter her rented apartment
without looking, without seeing.
Her diploma hangs in the hallway,
and these Florentine women,
all *casalinghe*, don't know. Always
rushing, talking, they take off
their shoes. They don't know

silence is needed to walk the way
of the flowers. While they're having
pranzo, prosciutto and pasta,
Keiko sits with bent branch,
scissors, pebbles, & her bridge.

PIANURA PADANA

That year, I traveled five thousand years to Tuscany,
to live with a man from Fiesole who sold door handles
to Ferramenta stores. We went to Assisi, San Gimignano,
Milano, Ferrara, drove to Arezzo through cypress trees-lined
roads, saw Petrarch's home, drank brunello, decanted
and slightly warmed. One weekend in February
we walked along paths on top of city walls
that Ercole d'Este commissioned in Ferrara.
From our hotel balcony I watched a woman bike
along the Po, her legs hidden by fog. I remember
her long hair, red bike handles, torso floating on clouds.
We hadn't been together centuries, the lying had not
started yet, though I already felt like getting on an eagle
and flying home, except there was no "nest" for me,
not with my mother and her second husband, not
with my first husband and his anger. The lying
had not yet started, but part of me, like the woman
on the bike—felt invisible, polluted like the waters of the Po.

PORTRAIT OF A YOUTH: LUCREZIA BORGIA DUCHESS OF FERRARA

I can hold what's left of her hair, what Byron didn't take,
read her letters, recite the Spanish poem
she copied out by hand, open the locket she used to wear,
"est animum" carved on it, the way Bembo asked.
I can wear her gold rings, read St. Matthew,
drape her shawl across my shoulders. But even then,
I wouldn't know her. I wonder why the young Lucrezia
in this portrait makes me uneasy. It's not
the Venusian myrtle shrub behind her, white flowers
sprinkled on the canvas, nor the words "honor and loyalty"
written on the paper in the painting. It's not
her blond hair—long and loosely curled
in other portraits—now pulled back and braided,
and it's not her face, beautiful, and so much like a boy's,
with rosy cheeks, and lips, small, and full, almost
pouting, as if she might start crying at any moment.
It's not the dagger either, or the way she holds it
in the portrait, one hand suspended above
the round handle carved into a golden flower
—a reference to the other Lucrezia, who plunged
a dagger in her chest after a king's son raped her.
What it is, is the infinite sadness in her large, dark,
almond eyes, looking at me, trying to tell me something.
What it is, is her sadness speaking to my sad almond eyes.

If this is her, painted by Dosso Dossi in 1516,
she was thirty-six, three years away from dying,
which means, she'd suffered through her loves and hates.
I too have had three husbands, though my father

didn't choose them, and my brother didn't kill
the one I loved. I too gave birth to children, though
not to eight, four of which she lost. Imagine her,
Lucrezia Borgia, Duchess of Ferrara, at thirty-nine
lying on her bed for days. It's late afternoon, June.
The Duchess, pale as usual, her forehead moist and sticky
from the sweat. A nurse soaks linen cloths in water,
spreads them on her chest. All evening she will lay here
in silence, mumbling, asking for water.
Tomorrow, at dawn, before she flies away,
she'll hear the swallows sing outside her window.

HONEYMOON IN ISCHIA

How small the island was, how hilly,
how cold in May. They took the child
with them, to the sunny terrace,
the terracotta tiles, sun on the tiles,
and from the hotel, a clear
view of the Tyrrhenian Sea.
She remembers driving down
the hill into town for dinner,
but has forgotten where they ate,
what red wine they drank,
what they talked about.
She doesn't remember making love,
but she remembers the terrace
had French doors, kept open
so she could breathe in the sea air.
So she could breathe. The wedding
dress was white, short, and tight.
At Ponte Vecchio, her light raincoat
couldn't keep her warm. Ischia
must be beautiful on hot summer days,
the crowds at the beach, the beach umbrellas.
In her favorite wedding picture
her daughter drinks milk from a bottle,
green eyes shaped like white grapes.
In another one she's getting out
of the Mercedes—a straniera,
more mistress than wife,
more girlfriend than mistress,
wearing sunglasses, red lipstick.
Next to her chaise on the hotel terrace
she spreads a towel, and on the towel
places her daughter's coloring books

and coloring pencils. Soon they'll take
the ferry back to Naples and drive back
to Tuscany where she'll start her married
life. Stefano has gotten lost in the crowd
that came out to see her marry him,
a duke's grandson, a true *signorino*.

IL MIO MARITO ITALIANO

Nessuno sa quando parte l'amore (sometimes I think in Italian).
Spring mornings in front of our window: hills, vineyards,
back roads. Behind me, our empty bed, rumpled sheets
smelling of sweat, pillows, blankets.
He painted our bedroom walls white, the trim blue,
covered the mattress with rose colored sheets,
chained it to the ceiling under a mosquito net.
Empty bed where we first lay, where I discovered his skin
—soft as a woman's, hard underneath, discovered his beauty,
his Tuscan villa, fragrant grapes, his Santa Cristina,
his room, his presents, his love-makings and whisperings,
his Milanese accent, his gold ring, his listening to my stories
—half in Italian, half in Spanish, about life as a young wife
in America, about other men. All discoveries. At night,
after drinking Vin Santo, he climbs on the bed, rocks
in mid-air, seasick. I stand by the window, study
the darkness of the open night, and for an instant forget
his lies, his screams, his gun, his stories about photographs
she left behind, about *her*, drunk, driving her Skoda
into the rain. I want to ask. Was this also *her* bedroom?
Also *her* bed? How long had *she* been gone when we met?

WHAT I NEVER TOLD YOU
ABOUT THE MARRIAGE

That at the beginning, I had no intention of lying.
That when people said it would never last,
I thought they were wrong.
That before the ceremony I doubted my feelings
but married you anyway.
That on the day of the marriage I wore white
for the part of me that wants to be pure,
a short dress for the other part.
That Elisabetta made my bouquet
with roses from the garden.
That Daria and I improvised a veil
from your daughter's first communion dress.
That I let Monica put more make-up on me
than I'll ever wear again.
That I enjoyed being driven to il Municipio
and around the piazza by Claudio
in his Mercedes convertible.
That while walking up the steps in town hall
I doubted my feelings.
That at the beginning, I had no intention of lying.
That the first time you accused me, you were
wrong. That I believed what you said
about your ex-wife, how she drank,
neglected the children, took valium.
That after I found the reports of her hospital stay,
I thought you had broken her arm.
That the first time you screamed me awake
in the middle of the night,
love diminished. That I knew
where you kept your handgun. That I hid
my passport in a safety deposit box in the bank.
That at the beginning, I had no intention of lying.

EARLY FALL IN THE BOBOLI GARDENS

Strolling down Viale Petrarca, heat on our arms,
heat on our faces, heat on the large iron gates
in Porta Romana. Children ride tricycles,
throw soccer balls, and play with sand,
their hands, shoes, hair, covered in dust.
"Ma come è brava" a mother boasts
about her daughter's sand cake.
And everyone claps. Next to them,
on blankets spread out on the grass,
two mothers breastfeed. Children
eat snacks. Most days, I sit with them
but today I wheel my daughter in her stroller
along the wide promenade up to the fountain
and the stone putti staring at us.
Did Dante walk here, Oltrarno? Did he cross
Ponte Vecchio and Via Porta Romana
on his way to San Miniato? It's Friday,
breezy afternoon. A blonde woman tossing coins
whispers words in another language. My daughter
looks at her and holds her hand out.
I unfasten her belt, run my hand along the bottom
of my purse fishing for lire. "Mamma! Ora tu."
In these gardens in Florence, I don't know
who I am, what to wish for. It's 1991.
It's four o'clock in the afternoon.
I've been in this city five years.
The manicured gardens, perfectly sculpted
stone gods, the boxwood mazes comfort us,
mother and daughter lost in Firenze, lost
in Italia, lost in our house on Via Metastasio.
My loneliness is as immense as
my determination to hide it, but my daughter

knows. Caught in the beauty of her green eyes,
I think, at three she carries my sadness.
We abandon the buggy, run up to the top of the steps
in love with the world and each other.
That was twenty years ago. We've learned
a couple of things since, not about wishing
and tossing coins into fountains or afternoons
spent in the Boboli Gardens—unlike the mothers
and children that day in the park what we learned
took us far away from Via Metastasio and the man
who was husband and father to us. Anything
I did, I had to do. If there's one rule I had to follow,
it's don't look back. Don't look back and don't let him
soften your heart. Never mind the pain.
Climb two steps at a time until you reach the top,
then run. Never mind all the dust your shoes will stir.

ARTEMISIA'S SUSANNA

For Susanna's flesh Artemisia prefers a bright pigment,
bathing half of her belly, her left breast and her right
thigh in light. No pearl earrings, necklaces, or bracelets.
She doesn't want a comb next to her, nor a mirror,
nor a silver jar filled with perfumed cream.
Instead of Tintoretto's gold-fringed shawl draped
over Susanna's ankle, the Roman painter
places a white cloth over the left thigh of her Susanna.
This year, in his new study in Antwerp, Rubens paints Susanna
sitting on a crimson cape with leopard fringe around it,
like a queen's, and an elder with one foot over the marble
balustrade, his right hand reaching out to touch her.
I wonder what Artemisia felt while sketching the old men
on her canvas, one whispering in the other's ear,
the other one trying to whisper in Susanna's.
They're leaning towards her as she leans away from them,
her face distorted, raised, the fingers of her right hand
closed, palm facing the men.
How much time did Artemisia spend on Susanna's hands?
How many weeks on each finger?
I wonder if, looking at them, she thought of Tassi's hands
—stained, cracked, dry—and shivered.
I imagine Artemisia concentrating on a strand
of Susanna's hair, lying like a wild wave on one cheek.
It must have come loose as she turned her face away,
mouth slightly open, as if about to speak.
How much time did she spend on the lips, full, pink,
and parted? When her father takes Tassi to court,
Artemisia won't have time to paint. For months,
she'll sit on a hard bench facing the judge,
her hands smoothing out the creases on her cape.

ELEGY FOR EUGENIO MONTALE

Tutto brucerá dans l'espace d'un matin.
During the breadth of a morning all will burn.
Your place in Via Biglio in Milan,
the apartment in Florence where you lived,
the apartment in Florence where I stayed,
the waterbed I talked *him* into buying,
the custom-made wood frame for the bed,
his uneasiness about sleeping on water,
his fear of electrocution from the heater,
fear of paralysis, fear of freezing on the bed,
cold waves rocking his body—queasy with
motion sickness, sick with knowing I wouldn't
stay. Jealous hands hurled my sculpture
across a room. The English chair in my study,
he gave away. *Tutto brucerá.* Genoa, my Spanish,
your French, our Italian, memories of your wife,
her illness, your Sunday afternoons
with Annalisa Cima, your poems, typed,
folded, sealed in envelopes and saved by Cima.
Tutto brucerá. Your poem about the lyric rain,
birth and death certificates, degrees, divorce
papers. I too am fed up with a world
that's *exploding already.* All will burn.
Airplanes, guns, poor translations of Baudelaire,
Botero's bronze, round women, though these
are not your words. *Tutto brucerá dans*
l'espace d'un matin, you wrote, but every day,
a little burning's taking place.

THE MASK

For Jiri Zizka

What happened to the Alaskan mask I bought
in a tourist shop in Valdez, along with T-shirts,
key chains, coffee mugs? Why did I buy it,
why did I give it away? Crafted out of deer skin,
decorated with light blue, red, white stripes,
beaded strands, feathers, it was wild,
holes for the eyes circled in black.
June light everywhere, evenings spent
at the Pipeline Bar drinking, dancing.
Light walking in, light leaving. Too much light,
too many sleepless nights, will drive you mad.
I stood in the small shop staring at the mask,
exotic, terrifying, and at a yawning clerk
who refused to say the artist's name, the tribe.
Where could I hang this mask, which for me was art,
for someone else religion? I finally hung it in my porch,
by black and white photographs, poems, canvases,
old tubes of acrylic paint. Like me, the mask
didn't fit in with the décor. I decided to give it
to my friend, who had a place to hang it
in his living room, next to his African masks.
Now I wonder what happened to my mask after he died?
Did it go to his son, his ex-wife, a thrift shop?
Was it buried with him in fresh soil, so he could wear it
in the after-life? And why think of that mask at all,
as if it were part of me, as if I cared?

WEEDS

Now, I sit at the window in my study looking at the fence
where seeds he gave me blossomed into *Prunella vulgaris*.
But that was many years ago. Now, the sunset covers
my West Virginia garden, spreading over fence, weeds,
flowers, memories of my friend, who said the plant,
like all weeds, needed a wall to climb. I grew up
in a land of guava trees, and trees whose names
I never memorized—there were so many—
I know the wild side of plants. In Manchester,
on weekends, my friends and I went to pubs,
walked in gardens. I learned the versification of flowers,
the harmony of order. I never learned to garden, though,
and I don't know why I bought soil when I got the seeds,
planted them, nurtured the weed. Maybe because
those seeds were his only gift? Maybe because
for a brief time, they gave us something to talk about?
Maybe because I wanted him to love me?
Now, silence spreading over what I recall
of our meals and conversations,
his favorite answer to all my questions: "I don't know."
When the first stem of the weed sprouted,
I took pictures to show him, moved the plant outside
(as he told me), next to the fence, next to the basil
and the sage my husband had planted. I dug a hole,
covered the roots with fresh soil, watered it. Looking
back, I don't know why dry seeds meant so much
to me, why I worked so hard at gardening that spring,
why I took pictures of the thin, flimsy stem
of a weed to send to him. Maybe I wanted him
to love me, to praise something I had done,
something my hands had touched. Purple poppies,
their silky petals like royal robes in Ancient Rome,

blossomed once. It was a beautiful weed,
hard to keep, difficult to bring back. Like him.
Behind his row house in the city, my friend dug,
planted, watered. I watched him work, but never
got to see his roses blossom. While he dug,
he talked about his mother, dead of a heart attack
at forty, about his father, who broke
his mother's heart, about his sister, also dead.
He didn't talk about his sorrow, after love failed,
after his marriage broke, but he showed me
a childhood photograph in the country side
outside of Prague with his grandparents.
Years after he returned to Prague
he got his Czech passport. Oh, how he looked
at it with pride, glad they had taken him back.
But the truth is, he didn't have a country.
When he'd called to tell me about the seeds,
he'd said, "I give my friends gifts that bring life."
Tell me, then, why did he die? I never understood him.
I thought weeds came back, even after you tried to kill them.

GHOSTS

After your brother told me you had died,
I drove around for hours, listening
to Dvorak's "Cello Concerto."
Truth is, Dvorak came on the radio while I drove,
and I took it as a sign that you were there,
next to me, quiet as usual. From you,
I learned Dvorak's music. In Philadelphia
—drinking Argentinian Cabernet
in a Brazilian restaurant—we talked about
Jan Hus's Religious Revolution, Soviet tanks
in the streets of Prague in 1968. You told me
how you fled in the middle of the night
with a one-way ticket to New York,
a stranger's address in your hand.
In 1989, during your Velvet Revolution,
I was living in Florence with a one-year old
daughter and a man. Antonin's concerto
reminds me of the last time I saw you.
Too late for lunch, too soon for dinner,
we walked around Walnut Street looking
for restaurants. How was I to know
that you were dying, that I would never
see you after seeing Prague? I kept the map
you gave me that day, notes scribbled in black,
asterisks, places I must visit highlighted in yellow.
I sat at Café Slavia remembering our conversations
about your student days as a film major, the university,
afternoons spent with friends smoking, drinking,
discussing revolution in hushed tones.
Perhaps that's when you learned to whisper.
Or perhaps it was after your mother and sister
left silent spaces in your heart. You didn't have

to tell me. I heard it in your voice, as you
showed me a black and white photograph,
the three of you, dressed in Sunday clothes,
except there were no Sundays then,
because the Soviets said there was no God.
Your hair was blond, you held your mother's hand.

Bethlehem Chapel, a sparse, medieval church
highlighted on your face. Facing a wooden podium
where Jan Hus stood delivering his sermons,
I watch the light, filtering in, softening the blues,
reds, yellows, on what remains of frescoes,
notice the dry baptismal font, abandoned,
like an ancient ruin, in the middle of the room.
I wonder if it was also dry the day your mother
left her house before dawn with you wrapped up
in silk and wool—so you wouldn't catch a cold—
to meet the priest who came to name you,
sprinkle holy water on your head, pray
for your soul, while your mother held you
in her shaking arms, knowing she would go
to prison if they found you both in the house
of God. I see the church, cold and dark
but for a single candle, the first notes of dawn
seeping through the windows, the priest,
speaking a forgotten and forbidden language,
giving your life some meaning, your mother's life
some faith. Today, under light soon to turn crepuscular,
musicians play Vivaldi. From my seat I study the dry,
baptismal font where your mother and the priest
once stood, whispering your name, praying.

Vivaldi's Seasons seem too cheerful for this chapel,
my memories of you. Long after the cellos cease,

empty chairs arranged in neat rows.
Outside, clouds float. A young, handsome cellist
places his cello inside its case, shuts it.
He wears black, like you did, his hair slicked back.
For a moment, his large, amber eyes, sweet, like yours,
meet mine. I envy him. He speaks your language,
which I never learned. I think of you, far away,
lucky to be baptized, lucky to know
your mother loved you enough to risk her life.
You were right: it's quiet here, pleasant,
almost peaceful. Adios, arrivederci, ciao.

THE BELLS OF ERICE

Today, bells from Los Jeronimos remind me
of a sleepy Sicilian town where conversations stop
and shopkeepers standing in doorways
wake-up—like the dogs, napping against walls
along narrow streets—to listen to the bells
sing, "come, come, come," as the sirocco
whistles past empty churches. It's enough
to break your heart, watching the saints
wait on their marble pedestals.
Last week, in my hotel room
in that small Sicilian town,
I opened his book and read Part Two
of "Sleeping Lioness,"—dedicated
to James Wright—in which Levis wrote
that someone tried to make the illustration
on the cover of Wright's book mirror
snow fallen in the shape of a horse,
but that it looks, instead, "like someone
wrapped in bandages... someone
who could not see out."
From the cover of *his* book,
Levis, wrapped in suit and tie,
full mustache and eyebrows, tired eyes,
face half shadow, half-light,
the face of someone who's seen enough,
done enough, stared at me as if to say,
"I don't know why I feel like crying."
For nights, lying on my bed in a room
with a view of the ocean, in a two-star hotel
in that small Sicilian town, I read Levis.
Outside my window bells and wind died down
and the lights came on in the valley below,
and I could see as far away as Trapani.

Levis's book is open on my bed.
I am reading it; everyone else
in this town is drinking Nero D'Avola,
laughing, making love. If they talk,
they talk about grapes, how the best grape
is ripened on the vine, how it needs to take
its time, like the best wine, how the best wines
surprise, like love. Suddenly, I feel the sadness
the poet must've felt. Hanging on the wall,
an abstract painting with a line that reads,
"La luna mai non riposa," the moon
never rests. Like the poet. Poor moon,
poor wind, poor saints, poor bells. Poor bells,
made of metal and sweat. And poor poet, wrapped
in pain, constantly staring death in the face.

CHIAROMONTE

For Phil Levine

Remember the day we tasted Chiaromonte,
the red wine of Trapani? Sicilians drink it
with roasted meats and aged goat cheese.
At Monte San Giuliano, we had ours with bread,
carpaccio, salad. In a drawer in my desk,
a letter from you, an essay Larry Levis wrote
about his days as your student, a signed copy
of your book with one of your poems,
"Black Wine,"—folded, inside it—
where you paint your life in Barcelona,
the daily burning of your words at dawn.
I wonder if you left the poem in your book
for me to find, or forgot it between its pages.
I see you, and your sons and Franny
in a small apartment close to Palacio Guell,
you, frying your brains with vino negro daily,
writing pages you will have to burn at dawn,
Antonio, the Andalusian watchman
who claims to know Gabriela Mistral
and Edgar Allen Poe—staring at the fire,
wondering your wisdom. You must've towered
over him, he must've looked upon you
as a child. I say this because you seemed
child-like to me last fall when we walked up
the hills of Erice, you on one side of Franny,
me on the other, shoes slipping on the stones.
Franny bought stamps, looked for presents
for your sons, their families. You weren't
interested in postcards, plates, or t-shirts.
You weren't interested in talking about

the weather, but you felt it, and loved it,
like you loved the Chiaromonte we drank
that day at lunch. So much so, you copied
the name on a napkin in your shaky handwriting
so you could order it again at supper. Of all
the days we spent together, my mind goes
to the Wednesday at Monte San Giuliano,
the taste of Chiaromonte, your words about Levis,
how you said he burned through women, booze,
and drugs. How he burned. And now, I wish
that I could see you once again, to tell you "chiaro"
means clear, the opposite of black, your "vino negro."

ESTADOS UNIDOS

ATLANTA, SEVENTH GRADE

A portrait of my cousin—commissioned in Madrid—
hangs on the wall behind my bed.
The girl in the painting stares at me
as if to say, *any* thing out of place could mean exile.
I'm twelve, living with an aunt I've seldom seen,
her sons, her husband. The girls in my school
shave their legs, wear miniskirts, saddle shoes.
Humid, balmy evenings sitting at my cousin's desk
while she sits at her desk in college,
I stare at books, write letters to my mother.
To please my aunt, I also write letters to my father,
in Wisconsin, asking for money.
My father, Robert Horace Maxwell, an American.

WISCONSIN SUMMER

That Sturgeon Bay summer—recorded
with a Polaroid camera— my father
gave me a bikini sprinkled with daisies.
I'm wearing it in the picture, in front of the trailer,
arms raised, head bent to avoid water
blasting from a hose my father is pointing.
Soaked, I've been outside for hours.
Afternoons spent at the YMCA in a chlorined pool,
kids yelling, lifeguards on duty.
Here, in this water, this summer, I'll learn to float.
At thirteen, I still don't know how to swim.
Afterwards, we'll visit Uncle Jerry
at the bar where he bartends.
I want to keep sinking in Sturgeon Bay's waters
over and over again rather than sit on a stool
in a dark room surrounded by men.

BEYOND BOGOTÁ

I've dyed my hair red with henna from the pharmacy,
chopped it off with a child's scissors.
I've applied for a job at the chocolate shop to help
pay the rent. I've walked home after sunset with men
twice my age. In my mother's eyes, anger beyond
the speed limit. To sit still means to give in,
to talk in sentences I dread. But even when she says
no tienes verguenza and her words crawl on my skin
like scorpions to disturb my sleep, my temper refuses
to meet hers, becomes a storm. Even then, I love her
with a sadness she'll never understand. The child I was
still floats in me half asleep, dreaming
my brother and the dog playing hide and seek at the park.
Boy and dog walked three miles home and missed lunch.
It was then I understood my mother would never yield.
At ten I drew a woman with a blue fish on her head.
The teacher said I was creative, "our next Botero."
Now, untouched tubes of paints adorn the table.

CAREFREE DAYS IN WILLIAMSBURG WITH MY FUTURE FIRST HUSBAND

We spent summer and part of winter
in an apartment above Mama Mia's Pizza.
It was small, noisy, endless narrow stairs
leading up to it. I cut a red-and-white-
checkered cloth to cover John's
grandmother's table, agreed to keep
Portia, his blind hamster. Winter,
the pizza oven kept us warm,
but come summer, even the waterbed
caught on fire. Too young
to understand why mothers hold on
to their sons, too blind to see
impending storms, happy and deaf,
we didn't hear the fear in his mother's voice,
how it rose a few octaves when she spoke.
All summer we rode his motorcycle.
John gave me his helmet, wore his childhood
horseback riding hat, two sizes too small.
I held on to him with one arm,
carried new bamboo blinds with the other.
This southern boy didn't speak my language,
didn't know how to pronounce *guayaba*,
guanabana, maracuya, mamoncillo, zapote.
He didn't know the names of trees
in my country, didn't know what I'd had to do
to get this far. But I felt a goodness in him.
He was different from all the others. Early spring,
in the Sunken Gardens—sunbathing on the grass—
I felt we were ephemeral, like good weather.

WHY I NEVER GOT TO MONTPELLIER

Intruding reader, have you ever taken the train
from Paris to Mulhouse in January, under a pewter
sky, strangers sitting at your side, you, about
to surprise the man who's been writing you letters?
And yours, whole pages copied by hand from novels,
essays, journals. He didn't seem to mind, you
practiced your French. What could you write
after that Salamanca summer, after he never kissed
you, after he couldn't bring himself to say goodbye
the day he started driving back to France? His Spanish,
like his heart, broken, your French, learned
from textbooks. Have you ever sat in a train hungry,
by the window, staring at the mountains while
others share bread and cheese, wine, Romanesco?
When dusk falls, does the landscape blur as the train
moves on? I took that train to Mulhouse, and slid
into the station at five, to find cafes locked up,
benches taken up by nighthawks, the homeless,
and their bags, women, working the night.
In Williamsburg, my French teacher had seen
the ring. Shaking a finger, she'd said—the way
she'd conjugate a verb, I-was-too-young-
to-marry. "Go to Montpellier, speak French."

WHAT I REMEMBER
ABOUT OUR FIRST MARRIAGE

When you took me
to visit your farm,
I noticed the trees, changed
to browns, reds, yellows.
I enjoyed sleeping
in your old room,
on your childhood's bed,
though I've never forgotten
the picture of the old girlfriend.
We were married
at the Methodist Church
at the end of February,
on a mild day. I got lost
on my way to the church,
and was late, ending up
at the Fire Hall instead.
The town was so small,
getting lost was an art.
Because we were in a hurry,
I rushed out, bought
a cream-colored dress,
on sale, three sizes too large,
polyester, down to my knees.
I braided my hair, weaving
baby's breath in my braid.
I'd lost my good shoes,
and, to my brother's surprise,
I walked down the aisle
in red ballerinas.
You didn't care.

You were glad I showed up,
baby's breath in my hair.
This was years before
I went to Florence,
years before I re-married,
years before my daughter
was born and you got engaged.
I remember the day
you showed me
the ivory envelopes.
Stamped and addressed,
there were hundreds
of exquisite cards
repeating your names,
the date, the time,
the place, waiting on skids
at the plant. The ink
was still wet on the paper
when you sent
the whole job to spoilage.

LEAVING MY FIRST HUSBAND

At first he believed I would be back,
and that he would open the door.
In the meantime, he kept his job,
adopted a dog without a tail,
soaked in the hot tub, and lounged
on the couch we had bought on sale.
"Custom-made," the sales woman
had explained stroking the velvet.
In the afternoon light, it shimmered
like silver. After four years, another
woman has learned to cook rosemary
chicken and threatens to fill his days
and his bed. She goes through the house,
gathers sweaters, pictures, and paintings.
Now there will be room for *her* pills
and *her* make-up. With a drink
and Barry White on the stereo,
John rests on the couch in the changing light.
In his hand, the pearl earring he found
while re-arranging the cushions last night.

SITTING ON THE STEPS WITH
MY THIRD HUSBAND AT 2:00 A.M.

It's cool outside, and dark. He takes a deep breath.
I love this time of night, he says. I pause, breathe in,
breathe out. The taxi is to arrive at any moment.
Inside the house, our children sleep. This is
my favorite part of day, my husband says, again.
I look around. Pitch black. No moon, no stars.
I like to sleep at night. Today, he made coffee,
drank three cups. I've barely had three sips.
My stomach aches. He watched me dress, undress,
uncomfortable in my body, uncomfortable
in my dress. This man I call my husband
has driven me to the airport, picked me up.
Today we sit on the steps outside the kitchen, wait.
Across the street, our neighbor is zigzagging home.
My husband waves, she ignores him.
Every departure reminds us both the time I went
to Italy for one semester and stayed nine years instead.
He visited me in Rome, took my 3-year-old
Italian daughter shopping, and came back
with a red dress, hand embroidered in green.
On weekends we go for long walks on the towpath,
my favorite time of day. We meander by trees I've never
learned. He pulls the Great Pyrenees past bikers, hikers,
children. Cleopatra is moody, prone to growl. Below us,
the Potomac River, always changing. During his childhood
the river was so polluted you couldn't bathe in it.
Before him, his father used to cross it from shore to shore,
without coming up to breathe. Sometimes we stop, look
at blue bells, a black snake frozen in the middle of the path,
a turtle. He's never liked black snakes. I've always liked

his hands, so white, his long fingers, at once delicate
and strong, his ocean-blue kind eyes. The way
the year I came home at Christmas from Florence
to tell him I'd met someone else, he picked me up
at the airport with red roses and a bottle of champagne.
Last year, he planted basil and blueberries in the yard,
along with the usual tomatoes. This was the year of green
peppers. Yesterday, while I was packing, he offered to take me
on a tour of his garden. He wanted to show me his plants.

FIREFLIES

For John

Evenings spent rocking on chairs on the porch,
listening to pool water swish as neighbors swim.
Summer heat on our sunburned skin,
our glasses empty. Scent of hay. Grass, soft
under our feet, warm water waiting.
Out of nowhere, fireflies, their conspicuous
bioluminescence, which is to say, their living light,
light in living beings. Inside their abdomens,
these small creatures carry cold lights,
scientific miracles of enzymes and chemicals
lighting up as they dance, helping them find
and love each other in the dark. Like spaceships
in old movies conversing in odd languages,
they use their lights to blink new messages
at night, to talk. They must be free to shine
their cold, efficient lights. Capture them,
seal them in glass jars the way children often do,
and they're gone. Like me, they'd rather die
than live in cages. That summer evening
centuries ago, we tried to catch them
with our hands, feel their wings against
our palms, peek inside our fists to see
their light. I didn't know that as a child you
sat on the same porch with your father,
watching fireflies light up the night, the sky,
his words, while he smoked, the German
Shepherd at his side. And you, how
could you know that in those summers
there was so much we didn't know.

CANDLE

After the call came, we drove straight to Wisconsin,
fourteen hours to his empty place, to clean out
his refrigerator, meet his friends, decide
which coffin would suit his body best.
It was mid-December. Close to Green Bay,
the landscape turned white, light reflected on snow.
His place was also snowed under: blank index cards,
letters to Madame Corinne, articles about Martians.
On his night table, his passport, and *There are
No Coincidences.* This is the closest I ever came
to loving him, standing in his empty room,
looking through his things, learning.
He was born in Georgia, not in Florida
as my mother always said, and he was five years
younger than her, though she claims her passport
is wrong, and in his passport picture he looks older,
worn out behind his glasses, emptied out, wrinkled skin
sagging, nothing like the blue-eyed football player
towering over my mother, slow dancing
in their honeymoon snapshots from New Orleans.

Yesterday, she said, again, "marrying *your father*
was the worst mistake. *El peor error de mi vida.*
"Light candles in front of their pictures,"
a medicine woman advises, so I light a candle
in front of them, dressed up and dancing
in a night club in New Orleans.
He holds her close. Even in high heels,
she doesn't reach his shoulder.
Behind them, on the dinner table,
champagne, unfinished wedding cake, candles.
"Candles are for the dead," *para los muertos,*

my mother says. I wonder, how many
should I light, then? How many times has he
been dead? *Cuantas debo comprar?* How many
candles should I buy? One for each afternoon
he spent drinking in the neighborhood?
One for each time he left? How many for the years
he was away? And what of those neatly wrapped
packets he carried in his suitcase?

He wrote to share the news from a Brazilian jail,
as if he suddenly remembered he had
a daughter, and prison could bring us closer.
The stamps on his passport, Amsterdam, Buenos
Aires, Spain. And now, in West Virginia,
his ashes mailed here by the Wichman Funeral
Home, as I requested. For months,
I drove around with him in the trunk of my car.
Late spring, to please my husband, we went
to the river, poured my father, one scoop at a time,
on the towpath, on the bluebells, in the water.

SANTA MADRE TIERRA, GENTE MEZCLADA
ELEGY FOR MOTHER EARTH

For Frederico Vigil

And now, in the light of dawn, I stand in front of the wall,
in front of the pile of rubble it's become,
catching glimpses of you, Mother Earth, and the sipapu
you came from. A breast, barely distinguishable,
two fingers left on your left hand, an eye,
a baby's arm, another baby's head, a nose,
a piece of cloth, the button of a military uniform,
feathers belonging to the deer dancer,
all blurred, handfuls of blue, red, brown, and what is left
of yellows, whites, and greens—images I painted
with semi-dry brushes—gone, dead, piled on the ground.
Like this unbearable silence, light falls across our wall
the way it fell on the empty streets of Granada
the day I searched for Federico's home.
How can I take pieces of stone, pieces of you, of me, home?
Where shall I put them? My fingers will get bloody.
Plaster dust will coat my shoes, my Sunday suit,
my hands, my hair. I'll feel it in my throat.
O, naked wall, looming over me like a burned-down,
empty house. O, loveless woman, I painted you with love.
Now my hands bleed gathering your bones, boxing your ashes,
heavier than most, carrying. O, Mother Earth,
already hidden under a coarse brown blanket to spare those
that could not bear to see your nakedness, brown skin
and curve, a goddess giving birth, because from mystery
we come and to mystery we return. The student
must've pulled the blanket off of you the way a jealous
lover pulls the sheets from the bed, heart beating fast.

Like mine. Last night, I dreamt torn skin, blood,
pieces of wall falling. I heard the grinding thud of axe
on wall, crushed stone, riotous uproar, chunks of rock
hitting the ground, deafening shouts, you, crying.
This was your house. This was our wall. O Santa Madre,
think of the weeks I passed drawing cartoons, mixing
black, white, and yellow pigments for *verdaccio*,
hours spent beating the paint into the plaster,
careful not to disturb the surface of your face,
dozens of coats of clear colors I added
with small brushes, carmine on your cheeks,
vermilion on your lips. Do you remember our first day?
By evening the plaster was so thirsty it drank up
every brush stroke. You were happy then,
as if your body—shaped by my thoughts,
born from my hands—were love itself. I kissed
your face, your eyes, your belly. Now, my empty bed
waits like this wall, O, unbearable silence, O, transparent
light of dawn, O, desolate Sunday, O, lost love.

THE RETURN OF ALFONSINA STORNI

Staring first at the monument they made for her
and then at the sea below it, and at the sun,
far away where clouds met water
and the breeze picked up in Mar del Plata
she shuddered. Alive, she had littered
the heart's borders with ghosts of lovers,
pages of poems, visions. She'd had enough
of the city and its men, and more of the nights
when her heart, about to burst, dissolved
inside her chest and, awake, her mind
performed its dark deeds in the dark
among dresses she no longer wore.
She gave her Self to men and sea gods.
I imagine her thinking of her lover.
Beneath the monument built in her honor
the sea roars, hits the rocks, wearing down
stone, sea foam blooming on moss.
The sea gulls which had, squeaking,
spoken the broken language of her heart
as they dove into the water searching
for catch are gone. Mermaids that sang
her lullabies until the sweetest sleep
possessed her body are also gone.
And I imagine that she saw, finally,
that the sea is beautiful but has no heart.
She feels particular regrets, feels
darkly that days and nights spent with him
robbed her of an emerald deep inside her
which he cracked without thinking,
selfish with desire. The mermaids are gone.
She feels a woman's vulnerable sadness
and some emptiness, an awkward sisterhood

with the world's sad women.
Sadness and emptiness are pain.
She feels pain in her belly, pain in her breasts.
Regret blossoms in her chest
and travels like a sea gull to her throat
searching for the voice she thought she had.
She knows she has come back to grieve,
alone, a thousand years next to this monument
to her life, her art, her loneliness.
I imagine dusk descends, and the clouds
surround her, and the wind tousles
her hair, pushing her forth beyond
this woman trapped in stone,
staring back at her as in a mirror,
beyond the rocks, in an arch
of incredible precision into the water,
a small dot racing back into the sea.

THINKING ABOUT LINCOLN
ON SHARPSBURG PIKE AT SEVEN A.M.

Soon, fog and clouds will lift like freshly laundered sheets
revealing Maryland's hills, trees,
fields, the bridge, and the Potomac.

We pass Antietam, where Lincoln sat imagining a future,
though in the skies his life—a supernova—
had run its course, was almost over.

Not knowing how much time we have, my son and I
carry our private wars inside, in silence,
before sunlight breaks through the clouds.

My son William's mind on college, Midterms, friends,
mine remembering my first time on this road
one October, years ago, leaves yellow, brown, pink, red,

wondering what the landscape looked like
in October of 1862, when Lincoln and McClellan
sat under a tent talking about war, neutral death.

I'm driving with my son, his cough, his anger,
—because I want a doctor to listen to his lungs—
make sure it's not his asthma, or, yet again, pneumonia.

Hands on the steering wheel, my mind returns
to sleepless childhood nights by steaming showers,
trying to soothe his raspy, barking cough,

shaking inside every time I heard it.
He's now a man, and needs the chance
to take care of himself, make his own choices.

Hands on the steering wheel, I think of Lincoln
and his general at Antietam. Close by,
dead boys and men, some younger than my son,

lie abandoned on the ground. Think of the waste of blue
and gray uniforms, think of their rifles, next to them,
the letters and photos, think of the unbearable.

NAPPING WITH STEVE ORLEN

In the picture our heads touch. Our cheeks are flushed.
My pearls hang loose, the emerald pendant twisted.
Your wink reminds me of August on the Mountain.
You said "let's take a nap" and laughed at my surprise.
"The secret, you see, is to not take napping too seriously."

Let's go back to the garden at the Bavarian Inn,
drink vodka, read poems. Let's take a walk on the towpath,
in early fall, slow, while you light cigarettes and smoke.
You taught me to mind the diction in my poems,
choose words to fit my context. I loved you.

Now I'm on a boat in the middle of a river
after rain. Lost. No steering wheel, compass,
blanket, book, or prayers. Nothing makes sense.
My list of things to do brimming with tasks
I have no wish to finish. *And then what?* You'd ask,

by way of telling me my poems were unfinished.
The other day, I found three house sparrows in the house.
I opened doors, caught the first one, released it
as I shall release my children. *And then, what?* You'd ask.
What else is there to do, but let go? When someone
leaves, we should no longer need to need them.

I DREAM OF ALFONSINA STORNI

In her hotel room, she's sitting at a desk,
searching through her handbag for a pen,
writing her last poem to be mailed
to *La Nación* tomorrow morning.
In her poem, she asks Death to tell *him*,
if he calls again, that she's gone out.
Why did you give the last two lines
of your last poem to a man, Alfonsina?
Didn't you once say you sold yourself for the city
and its men, and spent your life forgiving them?

ESPERANZA'S COUNTRY

Once, in a cab in Paris, I let the driver think
I was from Madrid. My ride was free.
All those years trying to be Colombian, a waste.
I am my own country.

POEM
STANLEY MOSS

NAMES
by Stanley Moss

Poet Esperanza thinks. Poet Hope dreams.
Esperanza makes love. Hope has a romance.
Esperanza nurses her daughter. Hope bottle-feeds.
Esperanza drinks Manzanilla. Hope drinks bourbon.
Esperanza eats olives and eels. Hope chicken fried steak.
Esperanza loves a *caballero*. Hope a salesman of doorknobs.
Esperanza says, "I am confounded." Hope says, "I'm ignorant."
Hope and Esperanza, like many persons,
are hopeless and hopeful.

Esperanza is waiting for her lover,
and Hope is waiting for the same guy:
Hope married husband 1, divorced,
then husband 2, divorced,
then went back and married 3, who was 1,
(please never say again, 'Easy as 1, 2, 3')
1 and 3 is an American printer,
2 an Italian doorknob salesman,
grandson of the Duke of Mantua.

There are societies like Esperanza and Hope,
where a man can have four wives.
Other cultures which allow a woman several husbands
in and out of her cottage. Merrily,
the more animal in us the more male or female,
perhaps the more thinking, too.
Some lion in us, some alley cat.
We speak about knowing our onions.
What about vegetables rooted or flowering—
the potato, flowering and rooted,

the Jerusalem artichoke, the *carciofi alla Giudìa*?
What about human male and female names—
I've never known a lady named Abraham
or a Sarah who is a guy.
If I called myself Sarah for a day, so what?
If I called myself Sarah for a year,
I would laugh more wearing makeup and a dress.
There is or was a theory: woman is a man
turned inside out.

Why do I walk downtown and uptown on the east
or west side of the street?
I make choices for reasons I don't know.
Esperanza is waiting for me in a café.
Esperanza, my middle name is David.
I regret I seldom use my full name.
My passport gives my full name,
and *occupation: writer.*
Asked by an English customs inspector
what I write, I said, "Poetry."
He said in his North Ireland accent,
"You should wear a flower in your buttonhole."
Will my next book be known or unknown:
Abandoned Poems by Stanley David Moss?
It's closer to the truth.
And yes, I've read *Hope Abandoned.*
Should the logo be the sloth, the only green mammal,
half rat, half monkey?

NOTES

"Ingrid Betancourt Speaks after Her Release"—Betancourt is a Colombian politician and former senator who ran for president and was kidnapped by the FARC during her presidential campaign. She was kept in captivity for six years.

"Confessions for the Guerrilla Fighter Upstairs"—My Aunt Lucy lived next to the house of a leader of the Colombian guerrilla group M19. As neighbors, they had a friendly relationship. She was enamoured by him, and used to watch him come and go with his bodyguards, wave, exchange pleasantries. He died in an airplane explosion on his way to Panama to negotiate with Colombian president Belisario Betancur. My aunt's reaction to his death and the stories she used to tell me about him inspired this poem.

"Tito's Gone"—Marshall Tito (1892-1980) ruled former Yugoslavia. My brother and I visited the country shortly before his death.

"Falling"—Bellver's statue of Lucifer falling from heaven was inspired by a passage in John Milton's *Paradise Lost*. The statue, which is quite beautiful, obtained the First Medal at the Spanish National Fine Arts Exhibition in 1878. That year it was cast in bronze for the third Paris World's Fair. When el Prado donated the statue to el Retiro Park, it was placed on a pedestal of bronze, granite and stone.

"Elegy for Eugenio Montale"—Montale's *Posthumous Diary* contains 66 poems divided into envelopes (11 poems per envelope) to be published after his death. He gave the envelopes to his friend, Annalisa Cima, and asked her to release each group of poems separately. Some critics believe Cima wrote the poems.

"Santa Madre Tierra: Gente Mezclada"—is the title of a fresco painted at St. John's College, Santa Fe, NM, by Master fresco painter Frederico Vigil. It was defaced by a student in 1990. The *New York Times* article, "Whose art is it? A Dispute in Santa Fe" recounts the story. I learned about the fresco from Mr. Vigil after meeting him in Albuquerque when he was working on another fresco at the National Hispanic Cultural Center.